CHRISTOPHER SUNSET

CHRISTOPHER SUNSET

GEOFFREY NUTTER

WAVE BOOKS · SEATTLE · NEW YORK

Published by Wave Books
www.wavepoetry.com

Wave Books titles are distributed to the trade by
Consortium Book Sales and Distribution
Phone: 800-283-3572 / SAN 631-760X

This title is available in limited edition hardcover
directly from the publisher

Library of Congress Cataloging-in-Publication Data:
Nutter, Geoffrey, 1968-
       Christopher sunset / Geoffrey Nutter.—1st ed.
       p. cm.
       ISBN 978-1-933517-44-5 (pbk. : alk. paper)
       I. Title.
       PS3614.U88C47 2010
       811'.6--dc22
                                            2009036198

Designed and composed by Gretchen Achilles/Wavetrap Design

Printed in the United States of America

9 8 7 6 5 4 3 2 1

FIRST EDITION

Wave Books 022

CONTENTS

For David Joel Friedman

THE STRAWBERRY

The pale yellow strawberry
begins. In the shadow of the ramshackle
pavilion, its peeling paint and rust-eaten
railings, it commences. It is white,
then pale yellow. Let's play in its beginning
the way children played in this pavilion
when the saber-like grasses were green
and pointed upward, not unthinkingly,
but without having to think. Pale yellow,
whitish green. What happens next?
Somewhere, there is orange and yellow-orange,
and pink, then it's night and, what's more,
it's dark, and lights are playing in the trees;
the city lurches forward with its white eye
fixed upon a pinpoint in the distance;
but something, in these leaves, is watching us
with ever-growing care, and interest.
It wants to see what happens next, too.

Little patricians are driving toward the sea.
They drive past the bladed fields in bloom
and past the fields where half-built gray hotels
stand for the city possible. They drive
in vehicles invented in the Year 1
past cliff sides and towns constructed
in the Year Midnight. The two silver towers
of Little Bricks Rice are metal painted
orange in the cylinder sun.

Here is the seaside town called Castles.
There are no World War II-era apples
in the trees in the park near the dry
blue fountains and peeling spouts.
But there are some World War II-era nerves
hanging off an ancient willow, hard
and gleaming as harp strings in the sunlight.

Who put them there? Who put the buildings
in the field, dead and intricate as seashells
washed up by a wave at night? Who told
the patricians the sea would wait for them?

THE BATTLESHIP

Walking past the silent warehouses
all the way to the port
to watch the battleship. Eating
a sandwich and drinking a coke on a concrete
block beside the battleship. Then,
stepping out of an elevator
into a lobby filled with sunlight
flooding in from giant windows
far above and away from
the battleship, to see it turning
in the harbor, pushed by seven
tugboats past the steelworks,
past asbestos castles,
and float, lumbering, out to sea.

Vapor trails bisect the sky
and it is two blue halves
and then they dissolve
and it is one enormous half.

You want to hear more
about the battleship.
The long guns of the battleship
rearing up against the sky.
How it bore its metal tonnage,
its munitions and incendiary,
monolith and multilith,
across the reflection of the clouds,

just one among a fleet
of battleships.

Lands a dragonfly
with a bright red thorax
on the spine of the book
I had been reading in the sun.
I am dreaming.

THE INFRASTRUCTURE

It is a city within a city. The salt domes
behind the Municipal Asphalt Plant.
The cranes, dismantling
the temporary roadway over the water,
made of red and yellow metal. At night
the statues come to life, green atop
their narrow obelisks. There is also
the double rainbow, visible through
the green bridge girders in the rain,
lions carved in stone on the basilica,
emancipation, and an effusive granting
of wishes by the countermen, brief suspensions
of the laws of gravity, a turnstile leading
into someone else's dream, which, it appears,
wanted also to be your own. Steel claws
drag wet leaves from the storm drains.
Once in a while, walking down the street,
if you listen, you will hear the plinking
of some wind chimes from a high window.
If you lie down lengthwise in the grass
you can see the cities in the cloud, ablaze
with commerce. If you lie back,
still as a virgin, a curio, alabaster,
might appear—the infrastructure.

ON THE PLAYFIELD

If you doubt, that's good.
It's also good if, like a bridge,
you're bearing up under enormous
tension and compression, or if,
like a tree branch floating down
a tributary, you are scot-free.
And what if you're out on the playfield,
just among the clanking of the goalposts,
subaltern, alive, just an asterisk
under the sun. The beacon on the skyway
is alternately orange and yellow,
like the periodic table of the elements
or the leaf green pages of the blue Pomona.
The lions of yesterday and the lions of tomorrow
sleep in the shade of the quickbeam.
The chain represents the lightness of the body
and the heaviness of stone. It is testing
the bounds of servitude and friendship.
But what of the Disclaimer, its insistence
that any resemblance is coincidental,
that the monarch butterfly is not your king,
that you must steel yourself and bear up
under it? You can't force it.
But if you turn your back on it
and walk down over the grass,
it just might come to you on its own.

TO SLEEP BESIDE A STREAM

Father Thoughtful and Father of Waters
stood beside the estuary, talking: "This, my friend,
is the boiling place, the place where two waters
come together." So placid was the glass arbor of the sky
at that hour, having spent the long hours preparing
and maturing the purple vintage they would now taste,
hand in hand the two, each hand on each heart,
and a white sail like a truce spread out across the far
reaches where the waters seemed to follow ever onward.

Yes! The waters curve like star steel. They succeed
exactly where we have failed. And when at dusk
it snows fire, they lie down side by side
and sleep.

PROSPECTUS

Along the shore, watermelon
sold from a blue shack, or a shark.
If shark, the fruit
has quills, exquisite, burnished
like a teak prospectus just cleft
from the tree. If rain-bejeweled,
blackening, then a building slumped
among others, green and pink paint peeling,
though loft homes for flowing gardens.
Taste it, and you will be unwinding
in its sweetness, banished from the abstract,
the blackening cables of the sea's collisions
just quiet now, tides in seashells.
Throw purple burlap over the icons
and the marble virgins—it is Easter for his wares,
ripe, banished from themselves, all doors ajar.

MIGUEL DE UNAMUNO

I was reading Miguel de Unamuno
under lamplight and under the tilting
heads of pink carnations, pinker
than milk but flecked with red,
each a perfect small bell, or blimp,
or calabash—each, perforce,
a small russet bust of Miguel de Unamuno
staring into the asparagus estuary
of the Tragic, its dark boats
sailing along toward Battersea.
And what if a little of that wind
that fills their sails should come in here,
and it does... and that breeze stirs
the periwinkles on the grass outside,
and billows in the curtains, and turns
the page of the book on the table,
and those small bells, those little lamps,
those meditating heads, nod yes,
nod yes, nod yes.

AN OVERTURNED BOAT

An overturned boat.
And look here, it is far
from where the kelp triangulates,
the large green lashes of the sea
that close upon an eye
that never sleeps.
Here is the abandoned substation
and the wires in the bramble,
and here in the gravel lot
is the peeling hull—once alit
with volatility, now a sagging mound;
once apportioned chancellery glass unto its gliding,
and the slapdash windhover was exposed for what it was,
or seemed to be—a trick of the night
finding dawn, shaped by its telephony.
An overturned boat, a mosaic
well within sight of the dispassionate sea
and its deeds, awash in neutrality.
A small item, a token, an omen
for impulsive children.

BEDTIME STORIES

Fear not, child, The Story of the Angry Tree,
nor Strands of Jellyfish at Dawn. The Tempest
Loves the Teapot trails off, and the prayer book
called Children Menaced by a Nightingale
fills you with tenderness,
as does The Teardrops of a Shepherdess.
The Parable of the Thousand Windmills
will end with foxes having their weddings,
far from the stag-headed inventions
of the middle twentieth century.
Open the book called Christopher Sunset.
The dredging machines are in the harbor
working on their epic, which might be called
Green Bridges. Grapes, ever wakeful, ripen
on the vines preparing the new vintage:
the end of a book that everyone may read—
but only a short section at a time.

THE OPERA OF THE CLOUDS

In Teaneck, against the east face
of the trade winds where the city meets the sea,
a stairway ascends to a graffiti-flecked seawall—
the blue and red flecks are peeling off,
the fabled sea-skate soars over green pinnacles
just out of sight, and out of earshot
the boatmen are calling, the deafening wave
is preparing to make its point, which up to now
had been a secret. Pristine
is the eglantine in the chill, because of the chill,
the figurative memorabilia in the ice-plant
just another source of pleasure—
like the huge, inconsequential opera of the clouds,
of the waves, of the leaves, of our lives.

THE ALLIANCE

A staple remover and a padlock,
left on a rotting green table
on a windblown strand beside the sea,
at dawn, at the notion of the bugbear sun
lighting waves cerise upon the waters,
found themselves beside each other,
found a closeness more alien than day
to the Nightwoman Onofra and her dark
apron stained cerise—Onofra... Onofra
Calabaza. A padlock and a thing
to take out staples—both bright and single-minded
in the dawn, subjects
of a common master—two alien things
in alien dawn, somehow in alliance.

KATHERINE SOMERSET

Drink the pot of white tea, O Darkener.
Reanimate the Prothalamion and celebrate
the betrothal of Katherine Somerset,
and with Katherine Somerset celebrate
the betrothal of all to a grassy
ambivalence, and a stony ambivalence,
and grass and stone in the untorn sorrel.
Below the moldering palisades
I arrived at a stairway long unused
by wedding columns fallen in the watercress.
And Katherine Somerset was there
by the gates of pearl that led to the water
and the white tea rose was blooming in the pots
ceramic and semi-ceramic—the sky
was darkening with sunset as if to say
that she is beautiful, Katherine Somerset,
Katherine Somerset the monarch bride
of that no good Johannes Factotum.

THE NEW ANIMALS

I put down the flannel book
and walked outside to see
the new animals. The mini
scoop and the mini pearl
slumbered by the lion-headed
milestone. The angry red
moccasin dreamed beneath
the jasper viewing stands,
and I dared not wake him,
and it seemed all of civilization
had rolled into a ball
of green leafage. Some said
only the pink religion would
help us, others the powder
blue religion. But the new
animals just slept,
dark with centripetal force,
and each a mascot for the ball
of leafage as night began to fall
on the new animals.

BEHIND TANTALUS, DAWN

Behind Tantalus, dawn.
In the dawn, the box kite
navigating high above the wind-socks.
And on the tabletop, the apple
and the plum; hallelujah, shepherds
carry lances of power through the buckwheat,
genuflect before the staves of dawn.
Hallelujah, vocalissimus, the tabletop
is on the box kite, far out of reach.
How is it then the shepherd tastes the apple and the plum?
How is it then the lumberjack is sleeping
in the asphodel, his broadax propped
against a sapling all in blossom?
Tantalus, they are untouchable—
but dawn, merciful and new,
is touching you.

THE BIG THOUGHT

Walking along the shore
and looking at the sea
the waves and the sky
made me want to think
some big thoughts.
So, stepping across the greenish
whips of kelp, the broken shells,
the polished pink sea-glass
and the little cold stones of Aristophanes,
I set about trying to think them,
but lo, none were forthcoming,
not a one, while the sea, its centrifuge,
old and ramshackle, just went on,
like a symbol, under great pressure
all the time, like a word, even
a little word, like one letter
in an acronym, or the words
inside an anagram, pushing
against the world, when all at once
something appeared in the fog,
a ship with all its rigging
putting the sea in its place,
far away, small as a symbol,
a big thought, just floating out there,
on the fresh, loud sounds of the sea.

PROMETHEANS

This was an invention
to light the way for the factotum:
small cedar splints tipped with chemical
paste and sugar, thin as stranded copper.
But who made it burst into flame,
the centerpiece of Hildebrand, the pride-horn
and the bliss of Fu Manchu?
All night it was sleeting
on the slate-gray cylinders,
clear plastic sacking was torn from branches,
but we keep the peace, strong as Sherpas.
We keep the faith, sure as incendiary.
We become children, that we might become
children of lions. Our lips find the way
that we might kiss our mother: Mother Earth.

THE BILLS OF LADING

Under the Pleiades
the derelict steamer
trudged onward toward
Eritrea. Jellyfish
tumbled in the sea
big as dinner plates
semitransparent
an embarrassment of riches
beneath her, the eighth
of seven sisters,
in their robes of supralunary
employ. And as a marathoner
wears a laurel crown
to face the stadia for anthems,
so stood the captain
on the helm as one
who triumphs, commanding
the entire apparatus
of the steerage at a touch,
his emoluments
promised in the bills
of lading, barnacles
jewels in moonlight
on the hull casting lights
on poetry and its radiant conjectures.

THE PRISM

The prism is beautiful.
It is a trick of light.
How is it that a spectrum fans out
like plumage through the fountain's spray?
It is amazing. But so, too,
is the hibiscus; it stands,
prismatic, amidst the grain.
It supersedes the expectations
of the tester, appointed
by calling-out, autonomous,
led there through the mazes
and the snares that they
have laid for him. That who
has laid for him? He sought
the moon; he came
to the flower. Now
the wind, too, is like a prism,
making all sounds otherworldly,
bending the hibiscus down
to meet his ear, which then will
seem to receive its secrets.

CENTIPEDE

On page 85 of the bestiary,
we find the humble centipede, partitioned off
from the rest of God's creatures.
It is over 100° centigrade where she resides,
in block after block of freestanding corrugated iron
shacks, each with a stovepipe, making it appear
we're residing by the coal-screening plant
of a tipple-works. The pollution produced
by the centipede is measured in ice-parts
per billion. She is considered by many
the trajectory of cactus, one at sunset
and one at pointillist dawn. But what
were the standing Buddhas doing
in the phonics book? What did we get
for reading this lesson, for vespers
lifting off the tender backs of prayer flags,
leaves in the mighty stream, and figures
arms akimbo half-obscured by columns?
The centipede is small by the rotting floorboards
near the closet, or stretched out
in the sky in cold glory, depending.

POEM AGAINST WINTHROP

Lug Winthrop through the ivy.
Then lug Winthrop through the rain.
Then half-asleep, in bondage,
take Winthrop up again.
Past the statue of the jug head,
and the blue-green leaves of kale
wilting like wet paper in the fountain,
set Winthrop up and leave him,
poised and still in similitude,
a triolet, while you rest.
If he begins to vocalize
insult him with a gadget
or strike him with a violet.
If he begins to cogitate,
opinionize or stir, then unpeel
his skin like old green paint from masonry.
Box him in with facts, then cube him
like a sandwich, if he calls
for the Upholder, eat him—
the borderers will still approve.
Sumptuous was the fleur-de-lys
before he came—reclaim it
from the Louvre of old pillboxes
and let it, half in shadow,
start to symbolize again—
the trivet on the tabletop
sans Winthrop.

KEY AND JOY

My name is Key.
My godmother is Joy.
It is my first real day.
The sailboats flashing
at the tips of the Finger Lakes
let the newcomers arise
at the quince-wood gates
of the fire-permeable community.
You can almost hear
the Anthem of Youth
in and above the trees
like raindrops of water.
Then let the polyphonic children
sin against discretion
by saying Yes to it.
I've been winding a watch
since time immemorial
but time has not waited up
for me. The opposite
is also true. And the ivy
hangs from the rain
in the trestles. Now
it is time to start
the strange adventure
called Sleep.

THE SEA AND THE BELLS

I walked toward a big sound.
Nautical imagery
(the sea and the bells)
through which passed
the Age of Seasons
on its way to a late
convergence. Sleep
and we turn into veined pods
that birth our doubles.
Wake, and blink like a glass coin
on a square glass brick.
It is the Day
of Anxiety. We are eating
jellyfish like children
are tall with adrenaline
and as random as javelins
in the Iliad.
Tropical plants
so big and alive with rain
that they stand up and walk out
of the forest and into the city.
And objects walk out of the ocean
and into the city. From the city
we can hear the sea and the bells.

RELEASEMENT TOWARD THINGS

As you turn toward the window
to begin your work, there
are the good things of the world
floating past silently: a flask
filled with mud and gravel,
a red pen cap, shattered bottles,
a wet tangle of fabric and fishing line,
pink shards of glass with rounded edges, a chair leg
wedged between a boulder and retaining wall—
and where there is no organizing principle
a kind of pattern emerges gradually, of its own
volition, like children, half
actuarial—a life
is just a couple thousand nights
of summer, the lavender asymmetry of sleep.

CUM HOC, PROPTER HOC

That swallows come to England in the spring
does not mean they bring the spring.
This is what they say—but don't they?
Inane to say so, but a man is praised
for the way he cuts a stone block
with the razor of his logic. Brueghel
distanced himself from this,
and placed a changeling prism on the u-brick,
let it repose against the evening light:
a harrowing, a harvest, a gold-colored lapwing—
Then to touch the filigree page
of the tri-book as it lies open on your lap
so the frontispiece is the first blue leaf
of the incendiary book, and the evergreen forest
never does not have its dark green needles giving shade
to sweep across its pages and add a secret text
that all things be brought within reach of the dreamer—
This is what they say: the swallows bring the spring.

SUNSET'S ANABAPTISTS

Look, the simple longshoremen
working on the docks,
like sunset's Anabaptists. For you
that means it's time to sleep,
like milk for children.
And you are pretty sleepy, after all,
having spent the best part
of the daylight hours with the bean
counters and the green eyeshade people,
tallying the weight per cubic yard of manganese,
flax seed and windowglass, jet fuel, moist hops,
apples and broken basalt,
anthracite coal, yellow pine and marl;
these have all been calculated,
and the heat of beeswax as the honey leaves it—
these too are known as the rushes lean
toward nightfall, pointing to the sea
beneath the ringing star of bells.
And if one, lucid as grass, could look down
from the reaching altitudes, what
paraphernalia would he see strewn
mismatched in the clover, what boathooks
and suspension rails, what stockyards,
what pageant of the gross and mighty?
But to look up as you're walking on the path
between two forests, one of aspen,
one of spruce, sky patterned as rose windows
through the needles, through the leaves cut by the sun
and shadows into the small profiles of children lost

and children to be, and the children we are to be—
then and sudden is to be those children
found again at once by mothers, bells
ringing in the ice storm, sounds to be followed.

Now it's time, perhaps, to consider
the wares on sale in front of the forest
before you enter there, and lay
your head down on a bed of leaves:
there, some statues of mossy urns,
lichen-covered demijohns; and here
are some giant-sized carved wooden ducks
veined with sea grass. It all seems
pretty useless, like dew, or even
the very forest itself—for indeed,
who made it, and what is it for?
And like the forest, the bodies of water,
sea, lake, river, and waterfall,
all have their spirits, half child,
half something else, shivering in the spray
like red tape streaming from the towers
of the Granite City which, thankfully,
this moment, is small and far away
as a leaf, and the leaves all around you
are small and very near.

WHO DO I KNOW NAMED XI?

A small black wasp
has appeared on the yellow-green
apple beside me.
It looks like a small, winged cricket.
Last night, I dreamed
that my nephew, eight years old
was riding his bicycle
a cigarette between his fingers.
A note to myself says
"Write to Xi." Who
do I know named Xi?
We were watching
from the bleachers
near an unfinished overpass
with exposed iron rods
poking through the chunks
of concrete. Some yams
appeared, as if from nowhere,
caked with dirt, and mainstream
pop songs flowed like water
laced with silica
from an open window.

CANTILEVER BRIDGE

And then we came to the cantilever bridge.
There in the sky between the humps
of two shorn green slopes.
It was humble, and humbly accomplished
its joining of negative landforms.
It was not the Three Gorges Dam, no
marvel, no emerald ladle from heaven.
Yet it was a total world, and it lent
itself to a world, with its shining
aspen wingspan, its friezes with iron
tooled sequins. Solar beer shined
from the waters beneath it. Dear
bridge, you've no dynamos mapped out on pink foil,
nor do you bear fearsome night plumage
nightly. But we came to you, and you
were there. And we crossed over you,
and entered the international district.

THE CLOUD ECLOGUE

The Cloud Eclogue pertained
to two clouds floating above
a meadow bristling with goalposts,
having left the rusting weathervanes
of Garish Answer, Pennsylvania
far behind; Tad Staples, taking
the dictation of their banter,
wrote upon a comb, recording this,
the minutes of their flame-licked
Stammtisch: "A day, a day, a day
when blossoms touch the concrete pylons
of the cloverleaf and clouds turn
northward, northward toward
the pantheons of ice..."

THE OBSTRUCTION BRIDGE

An obstacle course of gates, nets, sails
laid lengthwise on the ground, pits, hoops,
tubs; to cross the obstruction bridge
you must avoid these with almost unthinking
dexterity. You have a destination in mind,
of course: the other side, the turnoff,
the turnpike, the frontage road by the docks,
and then the tree-inflected lane that leads
to the old stadium where sugarcane is rotting
in the flooded football field; but first we must
contend with the flying pylons and conical towers,
the giant waving yellow parasols,
someone is playing a willow flute, someone
is blowing an oblong whistle, the little ones
are dreaming under the water lilies, and when
they wake they won't remember where they were,
nor have a clear notion of where they are.
And through the webwork of cables
one can see the tall ships, the three-funnel
steamers, the bright sails.

THREE SETTINGS

1 CHINESE RESTAURANT

A down-at-the-heels pagoda
set in the middle of a man-made pond
greenish, surrounded by egg-shaped
rock formations tall and gray with rounded tops,
a footbridge with fake metal bamboo handrails,
a trinket vendor, some trash among the water features,
a duck, some greenish cloud forms
slumping across the sky as reflected
in the water, paint peeling off the sides
of the floating structure, three tourists—
and on the narrow pier
one acrobat in gold-and-red pajamas,
wearing glassy headgear with hundreds
of little jewels and shining beads:
this the washed-out image
covering one wall of the take-out restaurant.

2 APARTMENT

A dripping ceiling
and a brown stain on an old floral rug.
Lamps with no bulbs and torn shades.
A pile of shirts on hangers in a darkened room,
a stack of empty picture frames,
telephone directories, old newspapers pinkish
in the sunset light in leaning stacks,

in columns, a warped bookcase bending
under knitting magazines and lion porn;
the number for one Nina Blackthorn Black
written on motel stationery; the piercing
smell of urine and the windows shut tight;
the grass in the vacant lot next door
rising in its tangled skeins up past
the cyclone fence and toward the sky.

3 ROOM

A dream is a room
where you live and sleep
with others, with strangers.
There is a dirty mop in a pail
of algae-covered water.
Moss growing on the wall
in reddish patches. A kettle
of tendrils and leeks
simmers on the stove.
Through a window
streaked with grime:
the tail assemblies
of yellow-hammers
streak across the sky.

NARCISSUS AND ECHO

Narcissus is a paragon of flowers.
But first she was a man
who took a walk by the waterfront
in a time of gradual darkening.
He pulled up a loose plank on the crumbling
boardwalk and found a fish there, circling
with unnerving serenity, ductile
in its element. How then did it seem
hard as plate, sharp as parallelogram?
One small swimmer in an endless pool,
dark as the pandect on wine by Dionysus.
And Echo bore her gifts of teak and marble
toward the boathouse where the magic boy
was waiting, and the sun renewed
the rainbow-colored grasses and the dunes.
Narcissus was sixteen years of age,
a new yellow flower in the sun.

We, men and women, are plunged
into life. A pebble polished
by the ocean. Bud and fruit,
dawn and noon. Brotherly love,
everyday joy, horrible loneliness.
Then sharpened, then hardened
sensibilities. Under the grape-colored leaves
the apprentice fixes a cylinder. Children
just won't sleep. We wake up, it seems
like a recurring dream, because
we have fallen asleep at points
along the way. And it recurs
nonsensically, like the spinning
white cylinders of cement trucks
at dawn. We close our eyes and brace
ourselves for what is to come.
Alarms chime in the sky acidly.
The stars of the zodiac crisscross
the sea-green ceiling of the rail station.
A yellow door opens. We act,
we participate, we participate,
we imitate. We build in concrete
on the limitless horizon, feeling the rain
that falls above the doll shops, on the
hillsides, in the promethean sunflowers.
Then it's just excellence, sailing
past the icy city in the frozen harbor
and the sun on new structures, wind
in the picture books. The hour

hasn't come, of laughter and passion
of summer when plum vines awaken,
not just the buildings nor the unrelated
leaves in relation to which everything
is near and unforgotten, for they too
are circular, and never really sleep,
so when they seem to die they merely
sleep lightly, but also your very own
life, sleeping and sleepless, dreaming
and dreamless, with its clear beginning
and definitive end, and everything else
a middle you wake into but slowly,
the sea with its serene indifference
no mother and no father, but near
and unforgotten and in relation to which
you may remember them, as they always
were and as you are, half awake but
waking, not asleep but dreaming
of the endless city of cathedrals.

FAMILY PORTRAIT

The family portrait is oddly foreshortened,
making my hand appear to have a hundred fingers,
fanned out over my daughter like a giant leaf.
My wife is beautiful, her hair is black and straightened,
shorn like plum leaves by grape scissors.
Our son isn't born yet. The wall is green
behind us, we are seated on a red couch.
My tie is silver-gray, it too looks foreshortened,
spreading like a patterned sail over my lap.
Our daughter is held between us. Where mother
and father smile, eager to please, her eyes
are hard, despotic. She is two years old.
Her hand is on my monster hand
and my wife holds two of her small fingers
in a delicate pincer grasp. My giant hand
seems to belong to my daughter, seems
to be coming out of her sleeve.
There is a white light behind us,
as if a sun were rising in a green sky
behind and over a horizon which is us.

THE GOSPELS AND THE FABLES

We awoke in a valley filled
with unfinished domes. You
had gold highlights in your hair.
There was a time when all the fables
were newly minted, and picking bee heads
from the clover honey meant something
big would happen in your life.
Maybe ice would be kind. And maybe
an army of boys in yellow shirts
would storm the pavilions, then stack
finger-sized mummies to the sky.
The Gospels are a love story.
But this love is more than we can
stand. And we can play like language
with what we are, and what we mean,
which are the same, and different.
So we reinvent it in our image,
which is smaller, or no image at all,
or irrelevant, like raindrops
on the water-cooled aloe.

WASPS OF SUNSET

It's only an August afternoon.
The silver train passes under the blue bridge
without a sound.
A white airplane comes out of a cloud.
A great spool rises from the shining lagoon.
And under a tree by the shoreline, kids
whack at a hornet's nest with a stick.
It hangs from a branch like a brown, withered head.
Black wasps climb out of the mouth and fly away.
Clover grows wild around the rusting goalposts.
And in the sky—a white and silver sunset.

THE YEAR OF SLEEP

Is this the annus mirabilis?
The stingrays float like banners
through the sea. Over the sea.
For the sea is the stronghold
in the middle of a boundless forest,
as silent as sleep. And sleep,
as lived through by sleep's disciples,
is growing loud, and louder,
until nothing, not the plover,
not the dreamer, is allowed
to have it. This is how we vilified
the sea, vilified sleep.
And we were sleeping and waking
endlessly through a year of marvels,
the barracuda floating like a yellow stencil
over the sun. This is the year of sleep.

THE WINDMILL PAMPHLET

I found a small, matchbook-sized pamphlet
comparing the corporation to a windmill.
It mentioned the big blades turning uselessly
in the sky and the shift manager standing
in the grass in blue bespoke suit and tie
with a casual vigilance, a braid
of red crows just floating above a fat
hill. The pamphlet made me think, "Yes,
they have a point, what indeed is the
corporation doing? And if it is, indeed,
a windmill, what, in its workings, is my
analogue? Am I the wind pushing it?
The sails spun downward by the crow-ridden
breeze? The pressing of the fulling hammers
in the cold stream?" It was an unfinished
conceit, and my place in it was left open.
A shape appeared behind the shoulder-high
asbestos wall of my workstation. I
shoved the little book in my pocket
as he passed in his nickel-plated wingtips,
and turned my thoughts back
to the collectivity.

THE STORY OF MY LIFE

In a little book
the size of a new thumb
I read what seemed to be
the story of my life,
just in a different order
and in images—also,
it was told in colloquy
by two strange men wearing
white suits and sitting
in wicker chairs as they watched
a cricket match between
Lahore and Varanasi,
and these two men
had never known me.
But their conversation told
my story—the incident
with the triangle tombstone,
the plate of sliced guava
and the lock of hair,
polished rails in early rain;
the pink mail slip left
on the table in the phở shop;
tempests in thimble-sized
teapots, minor intrigues,
complaints, assertions, appeals,
an oil rig pumping
in distant clover, lightning
over tumbledown buildings—
the two men couldn't seem

to reach an agreement about
anything, and thus my life
went on, suspended between them.
One of them nodded off
and finally slept; the other
wandered off and disappeared
into a stand of trees,
and from that point I wasn't sure
how I should proceed.

SISTER DOUBLE HAPPINESS

Eating at Chinese restaurants
in a dark city at midnight—
Panda House, Five Oceans,
Jade Garden, Sister Double Happiness—
where the night bells
are tolling, and the waterwheel
is turning, and giant snow and spider crabs
are fighting, in slow motion,
in the murky green water
of an algae-covered tank.
In the small dining room,
too brightly lit, at one
of a few rickety tables
at midnight, we will drink
the oolong tea from greenish thimbles,
and it is here
on stained red placemats
printed with the creatures of the zodiac
that we will write our finest poems.

TO BE A BOY

Climbed a green boulder,
shagged soccer balls kicked wide
of goalposts that rolled out
into the breasting tide
when I was a boy.
And when I was a boy I
let me be carried
into huge, dark places
like churches, and the sea
where the squids had inked some blackness:
it was, you said, "To make
my dreams more interesting."
You too, my father,
were a child;
wisteria on summer wind
was mild, and it grew dark
in the dusty bandshell
at the overgrown, abandoned park
where kids played with chains
in the rusty maples. It was strange to be
a boy. We slept
in the burgeoning grass.

THEY ARE ALL GONE INTO THE WORLD OF LIGHT!

I remember buying blood oranges
on a cloudy day. A red helicopter
chimed above the seminary. That night
an opera singer stroked my hair
as I lay across his knee
and heard the sound of the sea.
And when the sharp sun rays of Lent passed
I spent summer in the high grass
where I lay awake with eyes wide open
not sure if any time at all had passed
and it seemed as though the sea in sea language
made mention of junk bottles and windowpanes
and how we learn to carry fire in one hand
and water in the other—
there are laws on the books
for whatever is the matter.
A fence ran along the border of the sea.
The punitive gates opened to receive me.
                                        O to stay
at the beautiful hotel again, whose walls
are covered by ceramic panels,
each with a glazed spring flower
winding toward a pinnacle
and shot through, daily, by hailstones.
And the small green playing-card bibles
of the street, the pink ivy and the golden
leaves, matter-of-fact and unbeseeching.
They are all gone into the world of light.
And it seems, once again, I have gone

like fog among the ice-plant of the sea
to sleep in the low shrubs of a Japanese garden,
with caterpillars patterned on the golden
screens (of life), and rain in the brocade
masterwork (of life), my hotel key
a hailstone in my pocket, the city
rising like strange guests in the sky behind me.
The presidential towers
interlock on the horizon, toothsome,
random as hailstones. But we two,
paired and well-ordered as the hailstones,
are just here, just for a moment,
informal, alive, nearly nothing among them,
the punitive gates rusted open,
overgrown with melon, dewdrop, and quince.

GRASSHOPPERS

I had this vague ambition—
that I would, somehow, be
just human. Human
as raindrops. The eggshell blue
helmets of the mounted police
reflect the sunlight.
A city is the correct and masterly
play of forms in light. So
is a grasshopper, one of which
we saw in the country under
the apple trees, another of which
we noticed like a raindrop
toy on the window here
in the city far from all
apple objects.

Let's recount the apple
objects, trusting they
will lead us back like flashes
off the tall and gently curved
Petronas Towers so visible
and plumed from cinnamon-scented
piers—things we never did
and never saw, whose truth
breaks upon you from glass
fables (like glass fables)
and have nothing at all to do
with them—unless to remind you

of what you almost knew,
frozen by the effort to bring them
here like strips of whitened
autumn grass.

THE BOOK ABOUT SPARROWS

That quiet bald man at the party
as it turns out was writing a book
on the innocence of sparrows;
the small and useless innocence of sparrows.
As pandas graze, aloft, in the swaying
giant grasses of the bamboo, trivial
bamboo, where trivially they are grazing,
sublunary, like children, beyond goodness;
how will his mind intervene upon them,
upholding nonetheless the beautiful shrug
of the still, unsurpassable sparrow?
Where a thoughtless shrug will bear her aloft
eftsoons above the perpendicular grass
and toward the pate of the yellow moon
and the giant night grasses of the moon.

THE BARRISTER

Today the Oak of Great Age
turned to marble in the ice storm,
petrified, angelic though
unreal as a bloodshot hammer.
So the barrister turned aside
from the Book of Holy Unbeloved
Sunshine, inwardly considering
the men and women he had marched off
to gaol, to the tower
of avid collaboration with the Real.
It wasn't an attack of conscience,
but a pause to follow a chain
of memories that ended up in Philadelphia,
beside the Liberty Bell on a day
like today, deep into January
on a visit to the colonies,
how the crack in the bell's
bulging torso seemed the fresh
ultimatum of the free, the Random,
shining forth from deadly bronze,
the evidence of human frailty—
a secret and lovely text.

THANKSGIVING

I've been puzzled long enough
by modernity and its poems.
It's evening. I'm walking down
to the river to watch the sun set.
The clouds are like millions of bright blue leaves
scattered across the sky.
I'm sitting in the shade of a massive tree
but the shade is alive. And under the sunset
the giant gray trestles of the bridge.
And under the bridge, and nearer to me,
shards of bottles and the gravel
of the down-at-the-heels marina,
its broken-down boathouse, the gray
cinder blocks in the weeds, an overturned
boat, a length of black tubing.
It's all coming together now.
It's the sky and the earth, resting together
in the unassuming darkness.

THE LAW BROOK

The broken laws lie strewn in the grass,
jagged and rusting like abandoned machines.
We are alive and free—early afternoon in the East,
and just late morning in the West, but first in the East
and then a little later in the West you can see
the new laws rising up over the horizon,
and children eating green ice in the quadrangles
of the city watch them, and the ocean's children
and the ocean's ex-children see them too.
But who are they for, and what do they mean?

Night has its rules, which we must follow.
Like children, we resist its gift of sleep.
Come morning, the sea leaves a jellyfish
cold and bluish on the sand, and a dead sea-skate,
and three red tentacles, a clump of alien grass,
a green bottle, a broom, a helmet
with barnacles stuck to the visor.

Morning fog is threading through the trees
on the cliffs and on the outskirts of the cities—
and new leaves are filling the branches
as if having floated down from the sky.
It's Earth Day, and the sound of water
flowing over white and rounded stones
rises upward to reach us.

(And I want to have a little book be with me like it;
a little book of the law with water flowing over it,
the clear cold water itself the law
with the small, white rounded stones of righteousness
seen through it.) (I meant "a little *brook* of the law.")

THE NEW YORK TIMES

The New York Times wants to be
a svelte, fur-covered hero.
He came across the threshold daily
petting a rabbit, a summer hare,
telling me his anecdotes—the wasp
is in the apple, the eggs are on the spit,
a man has built a triangular house
and hung it from a nimbus cloud.
Each day was tall, wild, and green,
and after he'd delivered linens
to the houseboats, and appeased
the little patrols, he'd come to me,
to tell me how the powerful
projected their will into the world.

You were stylish as sunlight,
New York Times, in great, leaf-colored
shoes. I had you over daily, sir,
while Mother was here; while they
were sleeping, mirrored tea was boiling
in rosy thimbles, we laughed once
or twice and the breakfast nook windows
phased into puberty, grew peach fuzz,
and blushed. I decided to end it
but you refused to disappear from this,
my so-called life. What happened next?

I wasted many hours on you
each morning, when my children were small
and were changing all the time
but invisibly, like little starfish.
Oddly, you stayed always the same.
And I lived in you, and through you,
you told me we should go to war,
and so to war we went—then
you told me the names of the dead.
I liked and agreed with and repeated
your opinions. I worked every day
in the shadow of your building
where I could see through open windows
into your offices and imagine what transpired
there to make you new each day,
the huge spiring clock a dead thing
on your tower, locked in a single hour.

ALONG THE PLATE-GLASS AVENUES

So we crawled along the plate-glass avenues
of the City of Windows, zaftig pears
and tortoises and shining doorknobs
all tumbling down the slaloms of the building sides,
the last egg-bent lilies leaning by sun-shacks
and the very rich unhooked from the rickshaws
to commence the mounting of the escalators
into the ultramodern, half-fictitious treetops.
What ghosts are stealing their Ferraris?
The wordless, the timeless, the transparent hours.

Who was roseate among the dumb bells,
dull as dishwater, fragile and cracked like a dish,
crabbed and drunk on apple wine, adorned
in taffeta stiffened with tree gum?
What ghosts are floating up to be with you
to feel the curves of the triumphal arches,
or standing on the peach tree ladders
always just ready to touch you?

The City of Waters, untouchable windows,
of lilies in the aspens, of the water-salts,
the fleshly, floral dials in the building sides,
the runners and the sleepers and the standers-still;
who among them could find you, have you,
who found themselves beside you in your fullness?

LANTERN

You were sipping something
like a cold block of cider,
the Zen skyscrapers behind you
and an ad for Lantern Cigarettes
hoisted to the sky where blunt lights
granted their prebendaries to constables.
Most of the time is a time of preparation.
Then sitting on the hill, where they
called Dana Ivy like a chime
from Sutro Tower. Am I remembering
correctly? It was the day that I
turned twenty-one, and a figure of authority
checked my license carefully. Forbidden
fruit spread its vines across the earth.

In the lobby of the Empire
State Building there stands
a rectangular black panel with white
lettering, an enormous directory
of names. You see, I went there
before the storm, and saw the lightning
rod, the mooring mast, the radio
antenna all studying the sky,
while golden plates in vitrines
in the interior hallways praised
the great concrete pourers
of the machine age. And then
this directory, with its neutral
accounting of the commerce here:
Penny Shemtob on the 77th floor,
Force International on 48, Hammer Pac
Incorporated, Misty Harbor, Dreamdrop
Productions, The Tea Board of India,
Westvaco Envelope, Josephine
Angevine, Chang Xing Enterprises,
Yocom Knitting Inc., Saul Ziskroit
and Dial-a-Diamond. A man
wearing an oilskin raincoat
scans the names: he's here
to see Louis Black of Regal Shirtmakers.
But through the revolving doors
the sun can be seen full on the wide
avenue. Purposeful men hurry by

in brown fedoras. The rain
has passed and the city
looks spruced up and bright,
a newborn day in 1935.

ELECTRICITY

Children picking through the rocks
beside the river on a spring day.
What are they looking for? Old green
net tangled on broken pilings; a couple
embracing on the tumbledown esplanade.
Some fishermen drinking beer from tall brown bottles.
Broken shells, tire treads, rusted aluminum pull-tabs—
downriver, near the sun, the great echoes
and the embers of the bridge; and upriver,
far away, the echoing spools and dynamos
of the dam, its forces crackling outward
like the giant snow crab's jointed legs,
like a web in sunlight, a net, a chorus
of embers, like a plan the river is planning,
abstract, afire and electric, glowing
in the levitating rubric, invisible,
visible to children, undiscovered:
Brace yourselves—electricity
is coming to us.

THE SABBATH ELEVATORS

J. Seery Mechanical is on Ivy Street
in West Hempstead, New York, according
to the hand-painted lettering
on the side of the white van idling
at the curb. A long white tube or pipe is bolted
to the vehicle's roof. The driver,
in yellow-tinted glasses, has turned
the motor off. He's sitting there, smoking,
waiting for something, or someone.

In dark hospitals far up Broadway
in maternity wards with tan walls
Sabbath elevators are running all night,
by themselves, stopping on every floor.
And in the lobby, a strange, perpetual motion toy
like a collapsible boxwood swift for yarn
that keeps unspooling. And florists
with rare and valuable plants
keep each other company, and watch
the cross section of an aspidistra
flower in the night sky.

SOUNDS ABOVE THE WATERS

We slept in a head-shaped
geodesic dome on a pier
in the shadow of Three Gorges
Dam, where hyacinth will kill
for dosages of purple.
An army of workers brought to bear
on uprooting the Clementine orchards
slept too, in geodesic barracks,
drinking Sanka from thermoses
on waking, strong as Navajos
under song-filled clouds.
We will apply their principles too,
in making cornstalks brush the heavens,
gem-clips hum along the spillway
or gaseous propane burning on the tips
of rivets, and thereby shall not wake
where they left us, but arise,
anywhere, like sounds above the waters.

THE WORLD IN LOVE

There is a red leaf
hanging in the sky
below which spread
the cities and the waterfalls
of this day to day earth,
and all the people
and what they're
engaging—and this leaf
is moving back and forth,
slightly, in a breath
of wind blowing down
from the mountains
like a great cog that turns
once every thousand
years. Would you like
to see it held beside you
and your life
which is taking place
inside the buildings and
machinery that breathe for
us outside the vacant
industry of the wet
and shining forest, as free
as the crocus not to will
but arising nonetheless,
your life held up beside
this leaf and its most
inhuman red, that has
become a ceremony,

heretofore having been known
by being known, now
just listlessly waving
above the pointed objects
of the empirical garden
whose shadows rush
to meet up with the sunset,
which is coming—so surely
we feel it cool on our backs,
even now.

THE FINE PIN

The airplanes are trapped in the snow
like polished shell objects in an empty
gray landscape. Let them have their moment
of forgetfulness, the moment when they suddenly
forget their function, for a moment, and the red
shipping containers in the snow are toys
for the mind apart from what they are, and do.
A refinery looming through the fog reminds me
of something. We shall make space
for the sunflower, the snapdragon, the doll
and the spectacles, and the unnamed kiln-dried product
stacked up on the freight cars. Let this
be their awakening, who towered up in sleep's
high elevations, to be brought down to where we live,
with fresh young leaves and their unknowable rapidity,
the sun's silver-white dawning on our presence
which is where we recognized ourselves in them,
fully formed, standing with alacrity, fine as a pin,
and it is good that darting tadpoles still
can fill a pond with light, suggest the future,
the summer, is an entity just at hand.

THE FIGURINES OF PEACE

This is no agrarian paradise.
It might just be five solid minutes
of leaves. When the trees
have been turned into figurines
of peace, and the people
have been turned into figurines
of peace, and the animals
are figurines of peace
and neither break nor poke
jaggedly along the skyline
but are clean and rounded
as ideas, or figurines of peace;
and the aloe's ice-green tentacles
spill across the skyway that spans
the great Lake Pontchartrain
while clouds seethe around the blushing
limbs that bear the water-cherries
upward into contemplation;
then those few minutes with the leaves
extend into forever, abstract,
each one a thing that had
to be lived through, had to
be endured, and had to be
changed, that had to rise
and fall, until still,
until seeming to have been
always still, forever.

THE JUPITER SYMPHONY

Little man playing French horn
on a clover leaf at sundown,
are you just another one of Mother
Nature's tactics as she strives
to flood us with the Specter of Disbelief?
And lo, just as the meadowed slopes
of the Matterhorn are flooded
in April by the Flowers of Disbelief,
you can hear its music, prodigious,
like looking out across the gables,
like the Jupiter Symphony. Here
in the city, I befriend subprefects,
wear levitical hats with many edges.
If it's wisdom you want, then go
to the mountains. If it's love,
stay, patiently, there where you are.

THE NEW MILLENNIUM

We somehow made it
through the twentieth century.
Now the new millennium
is floating gently above us
like a kite upon which someone
has painted a butterfly.
And we're down at the estuary,
muddy after the rains,
and golden leaves are pouring
from the culverts. The wind
is perfect. Our kite
is climbing higher
up toward the clouds
and we can barely see it.
And past the pasteboard station
where they store the water machines
and out over the waters
the hunched forms of the mountains
seem to be waiting.

SUNFLOWER

The dedicatory sonnets, so long and awful
are strewn in the dedicatory stalks, tall and green.
You might never finish reading them.
So let the grass have the grass books
and let the sunflower grow to lofty heights,
rank and grizzled, until someone names it
Dragon Seapath. And Dragon Seapath, the curmudgeon
prickly pear of sun, might overshadow all
because she is just in front of the sun. You might
feel that your apprenticeship has just begun
and all you do has already been done.
Easy it was to wash my braid in the fountain
where the naiads presided, the time at hand
for the unsealing of the orders. But mind,
it's not thick and unavailing as a Septuagint,
nor ten thousand warring rainbows described
in three words in an epigram. And though
the sunflower too is in the epigram,
all the epic war harps have been broken,
and the sunflower stands, green and yellow,
unnamed, just nodding in the August wind.

THE VISITORS CENTER

A book about nothing—yes.
And you can fall asleep while reading it.
There are six hundred kinds of roses,
a handful of apples in the coral
drawn up from the salt water.
A yellow tree. The tram will take us
far from the obsidian visitors center,
explain evergreens, deep into a wood
divided from a modern highway
and past a snuff mill,
where the friends we haven't seen for ages
are standing on the footbridge
in twentieth-century period costume.
The tamaracks are decked in blue-black bunting
for the sentinels, the glockenspiel strikes five,
and far away a cup of tea with bergamot
awaits your waking.

MYTHS ABOUT THE PRESENT

And if these are not the finest poems
then they are, at least, the present poems.
They begin the sestiad with something small,
like burdock or convolvulus, but twine
around the poles of the abandoned nursery
like burdock or convolvulus unweeded.
No shepherds meditating under catkins
in fields at dawn with foresters nearby.
If cobble trails are winding through the ruins
take down the ruins, superadd the grass.
The Lock-lender and the Preceptress are here,
as cold and passive-aggressive as the sea
to tell us their myths about the present.
But we need to let it multiply, even
a tumbledown bricolage of addings,
like the present leaves, the present children;
as the present rainbow, so the present rain,
so invoked unto the limit of undoing,
thereunto so done. In superintendency,
its ascendancy, its laving, its life.

This sky, vast and beloved of Octobrists,
says more than we do, or want to; and tells us,
perhaps, more than we want to know.
The fuchsia, open by the fanlight,
is operatic. Beside the river
the sawtooth fronds of the aloe
are green. As for spring, the dawn.
Sacrosanct and gentle, round like the Earth
is the Wheel of Friendship. The thousand-year-old
oaks are children. Sergeant's weeping hemlocks
line the path that leads to the glass house.
I am matching wills with a great gray suspension bridge,
its network of steel nerves versus mine of grass.
The river flows below us, unknowing.
Eventually, it will meet up with the sea.
But first it will flow by the Trees of Unknowing,
which are magnolia, aspen, sycamore,
and eucalyptus. Their leaves are turning,
but gently, like the pages of the Johannine Gospel.
Your friend, the sea, can hear us coming.
"I sleep," he seems to say, "but my heart is awake."

ACKNOWLEDGMENTS

Some of the poems in this book first appeared in
*The Literary Review, Crowd, Carnet de route, 751, Fou,
Washington Square,* and *Sententia.* I would like to express
my thanks to the editors of these journals.

I would also like to express my gratitude to Matthew
Zapruder for being a generous, supportive, and amazing
editor; to Joshua Beckman; and to Tom King for first
reading and commenting on this manuscript. Thank you
Maria, Elaine, and Samuel. Thank you Henry Vaughn. And
thank you Sandy Brown.